THE ART OF

Korea

A BOOK OF POSTCARDS

Pomegranate

SAN FRANCISCO

Pomegranate Communications, Inc.
Box 6099, Rohnert Park, CA 94927
800-227-1428
www.pomegranate.com

Pomegranate Europe Ltd.
Fullbridge House, Fullbridge
Maldon, Essex CM9 4LE
England

ISBN 0-7649-2145-2
Pomegranate Catalog No. AA160

Pomegranate publishes books of
postcards on a wide range of subjects.
Please contact the publisher for more information.

Cover designed by Gina Bostian
Printed in China
11 10 09 08 07 06 05 04 03 02   10 9 8 7 6 5 4 3 2 1

To facilitate detachment of the postcards from this book, fold each card along its perforation line before tearing.

Korea is home to one of the longest and richest artistic traditions in Asia. This selection of works includes a cross-section of objects ranging from the Three Kingdoms period (57 B.C.E.–668 C.E.) to modern works from the end of the twentieth century, in a variety of mediums. Such a selection can only hint at the true range and magnitude of Korean art. Here you will find paintings on silk, on linen, and on paper; colorful embroidery and patchwork; as well as stoneware, earthenware, bronzes, and porcelains. In each of these mediums, Korean artists achieved work of the highest quality.

The reproductions in this book of postcards depict objects from the Asian Art Museum of San Francisco, one of the largest museums in the Western world devoted exclusively to Asian art.

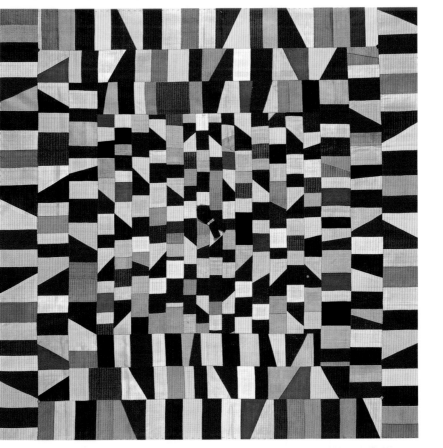

THE ART OF *Korea*

Wrapping cloth *(bojagi)*, 1930–1960
Silk pieces with patchwork design. 40⅛ x 40⅛ in.
Gift of Ann Witter, 1998.57

BOX 6099   ROHNERT PARK   CA 94927

Pomegranate

THE ART OF *Korea*

Cranes and Peaches of Immortality (detail), 1750–1800

Joseon dynasty (1392–1910). Eightfold screen, ink and colors on linen. 60¼ x 162½ in. (image); 83¾ x 173 in. (overall). Gift of the Walter and Phyllis Shorenstein Fund, the Connoisseurs' Council, the Koret Foundation, the Museum Society Auxiliary, Mr. David Hill, and Dr. and Mrs. David Buchanan, 1995.61

BOX 6099 ROHNERT PARK CA 94927

Pomegranate

THE ART OF *Korea*

Wrapping cloth *(bojagi)*, c. 1800–1900
Joseon dynasty (1392–1910). Silk with embroidery. 16½ x 16 in.
Gift of Mrs. Chung-Hee Kim, 1993.4

BOX 6099   ROHNERT PARK   CA 94927

Pomegranate

THE ART OF *Korea*

Rocks and Orchids (seoknan-do) (detail), 1910–1920

By Kim Ungwon

Ten-panel folding screen, ink and colors on paper. 80 x 20½ in. (each panel). Gift of the Connoisseurs' Council with additional funding from the Korean Art and Culture Committee, 1998.14

BOX 6099   ROHNERT PARK   CA 94927

Pomegranate

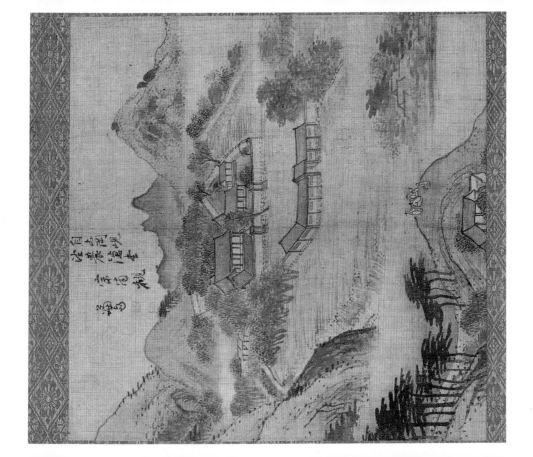

THE ART OF *Korea*

Landscape with Figures, c. 1740

By Jeong Seon

Joseon dynasty (1392–1910). Hanging scroll, ink and light colors on silk. 11½ x 11¼ in. (image); 42¼ x 17¾ in. (overall). Acquisition made possible by Dr. and Mrs. David Buchanan, 2000.42

BOX 6099   ROHNERT PARK   CA 94927

Pomegranate

THE ART OF *Korea*

Ewer, 1100–1200

Goryeo dynasty (918–1392). Stoneware with celadon glaze.
H: 9⅝ in.; D: 6½ in. The Avery Brundage Collection,
B60P123+

Pomegranate

BOX 6099   ROHNERT PARK   CA 94927

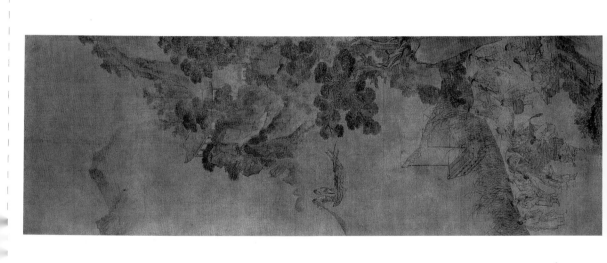

THE ART OF *Korea*

Fishermen and Scholars in Landscape, late 1800s–early 1900s

Kim Hongdo School

Joseon dynasty (1392–1910). Hanging scroll, colors on silk.
53½ x 18¼ in. (image); 82 x 27½ in. (overall).
Gift of Mr. and Mrs. Chong-Moon Lee, 1994.78

BOX 6099 ROHNERT PARK CA 94927

Pomegranate

THE ART OF *Korea*

Jar with tiger and magpie, 1890–1945

Porcelain with underglaze cobalt decoration.
H: 16 in.; D: 13 in. Gift of NamKoong Ryun, 2001.9

BOX 6099   ROHNERT PARK   CA 94927

Pomegranate

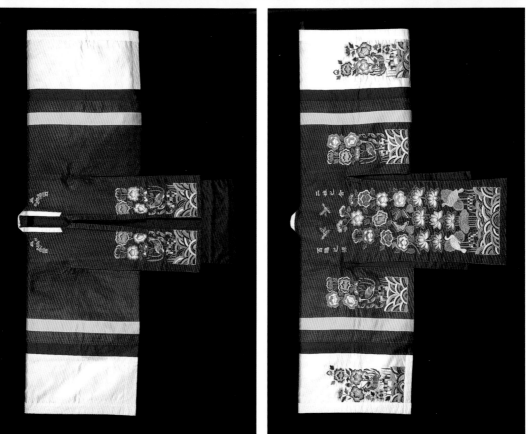

THE ART OF *Korea*

Flower robe with sash (*hwarrot*, Korean wedding robe), 1975
Silk with embroidery. 47 x 81 in. Gift of the Museum Society
Auxiliary, 1995.54.a-b

BOX 6099   ROHNERT PARK   CA 94927

Pomegranate

THE ART OF *Korea*

Duck-shaped vessel, 200–300

Three Kingdoms period (57 B.C.E.–668 C.E.): Gaya, earthenware. H: 12 in.; W: 15 in.; D: 6½ in. The Avery Brundage Collection, B63P13+

BOX 6099   ROHNERT PARK   CA 94927

Pomegranate

THE ART OF *Korea*

Prunus vase *(Maebyeong)*, c. 1100–1150

Goryeo dynasty (918–1392). Stoneware with iron-painted
decoration under celadon glaze. H: 11¼ in.; D: 7 in.
The Avery Brundage Collection, B60P17+

BOX 6099   ROHNERT PARK   CA 94927

Pomegranate

THE ART OF *Korea*

Buddhist monk, c. 550–650

Three Kingdoms period (57 B.C.E.–668 C.E.). Gilt bronze.
H: 4 in.; D: 1⅝ in. Gift of NamKoong Ryun, 2000.12

BOX 6099   ROHNERT PARK   CA 94927

Pomegranate

THE ART OF *Korea*

Lidded urn for human ashes, c. 700–800

Unified Silla dynasty (668–935). Stoneware. H: 9 in.;
W: 9¼ in.; D: 8 in. The Avery Brundage Collection, B62P24

BOX 6099   ROHNERT PARK   CA 94927

Pomegranate

THE ART OF *Korea*

Nine Cloud Dream (Guunmong) (detail), c. 1800–1900

Joseon dynasty (1392–1910). Eight-fold screen, ink and colors on paper. 34 x 15½ in. (each panel); 64⅜ x 161¼ in. (overall). Acquisition made possible by the Korean Art and Culture Committee, 1997.21

CA 94927 ROHNERT PARK BOX 6099

Pomegranate

THE ART OF *Korea*

Wrapping cloth (*bojagi*), c. 1950
Patchwork in silk. 23¼ x 17¾ in. Gift of Ann Witter, 2000.23

BOX 6099   ROHNERT PARK   CA 94927

Pomegranate

THE ART OF *Korea*

Jar, 1700–1800

Joseon dynasty (1392–1910). Porcelain with underglaze cobalt
decoration. H: 15 in.; D: 13 in. The Avery Brundage Collection,
B60P1793

BOX 6099   ROHNERT PARK   CA 94927

Pomegranate

THE ART OF *Korea*

Abbot Hyegak's Dancheong Patterns (detail), 1993

By Dongwon and others

Twelve-panel folding screen, ink, colors, and gold on paper. 101 x 22 in. (each panel). Gift of Hyegak and Dongwon, Tongdosa Monastery, South Gyeongsang Province, 1995.35

BOX 6099   ROHNERT PARK   CA 94927

Pomegranate

THE ART OF *Korea*

Oil lamp, c. 500–700

Three Kingdoms Period: Silla (57 B.C.E.–668 C.E.). Stoneware.
H: 6½ in.; D: 5½ in. The Avery Brundage Collection, B66P10

BOX 6099   ROHNERT PARK   CA 94927

Pomegranate

THE ART OF *Korea*

Plate with garden scene, c. 1800–1900

Joseon dynasty (1392–1910). Porcelain with underglaze cobalt
decoration. H: 1¾ in.; W: 7½ in.; D: 8½ in.
Gift of NamKoong Ryun, 2001.10

BOX 6099   ROHNERT PARK   CA 94927

Pomegranate

THE ART OF *Korea*

Bowl, c. 1300–1500

Joseon dynasty (1392–1910). Decorated *buncheong* stoneware.
H: 4⅝ in.; D: 4⅜ in. Gift of Arthur J. McTaggart, 1998.25

BOX 6099   ROHNERT PARK   CA 94927

Pomegranate

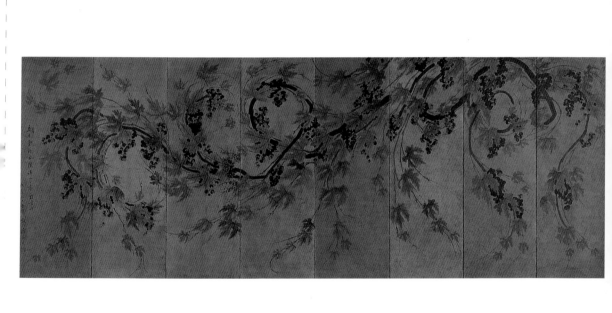

THE ART OF *Korea*

Grapevine (detail), 1870

By Choe Seok-Hwan

Joseon dynasty (1392–1910). Eight-fold screen, ink on paper. 74 x 15½ in. (each panel); 75½ x 133 in. (overall). Acquisition made possible by the Koret Foundation with additional funding from the Korean Art and Culture Committee, 2001.29

BOX 6099   ROHNERT PARK   CA 94927

Pomegranate

THE ART OF *Korea*

Embroidered wrapping cloth *(subo),* c. 1960–1970

By Han Sangsoo

Embroidered silk. 16 x 16½ in. Gift of Mary C. Stoddard,
2001.18

BOX 6099   ROHNERT PARK   CA 94927

Pomegranate

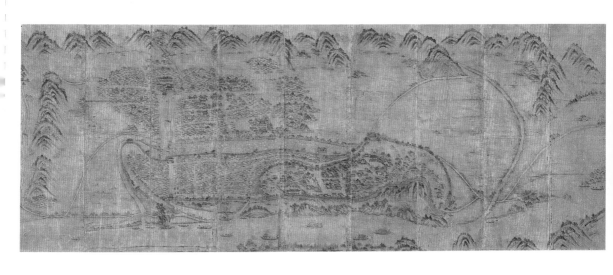

THE ART OF *Korea*

The City of Jinju, c. 1700–1800

Joseon dynasty (1392–1910). Multipanel screen, ink and light colors on silk. 52⅜ x 14⅛ in. (each panel); 52⅞ x 136¾ in. (overall). Museum purchase, 2001.1

BOX 6099   ROHNERT PARK   CA 94927

Pomegranate

THE ART OF *Korea*

Standing Buddha, c. 700–800

Unified Silla dynasty (668–935). Gilt bronze. H: 18⅝ in.; W: 12¹⁵⁄₁₆ in.; D: 7¼ in. The Avery Brundage Collection, B65B64

BOX 6099   ROHNERT PARK   CA 94927

Pomegranate

THE ART OF *Korea*

Tiger with magpies, 1850–1900

Joseon dynasty (1392–1910). Hanging scroll, ink and colors on paper. 39 x 29½ in. Gift of NamKoong Ryun, 2000.29

BOX 6099   ROHNERT PARK   CA 94927

Pomegranate

THE ART OF *Korea*

Wrapping cloth *(bojagi)*, c. 1950
Silk with patchwork design. 33⅛ x 32¼ in.
Gift of Ann Witter, 2000.22

BOX 6099   ROHNERT PARK   CA 94927

Pomegranate

THE ART OF *Korea*

Jar, 1600–1700

Joseon dynasty (1392–1910). Porcelain with transparent glaze. H: 18 in.; D: 18 in. The Avery Brundage Collection, B60P110+

Pomegranate

BOX 6099   ROHNERT PARK   CA 94927

THE ART OF *Korea*

Scholar's Accoutrements (chaekori) (detail), 1825–1875

By Yi Ungnok

Eight-fold screen, ink and colors on paper. 64⅛ x 13¼ in. (image).
Acquisition made possible by the Koret Foundation, Connoisseurs'
Council and the Korean Art and Culture Committee; mounting
supported by the Society for Asian Art, 1998.111

CA 94927

ROHNERT PARK

BOX 6099

(Pomegranate)

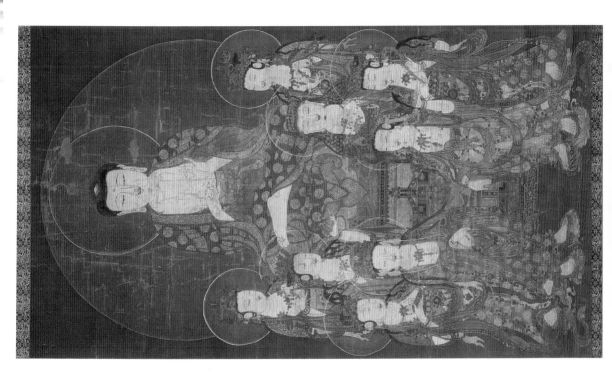

THE ART OF *Korea*

Amitabha Buddha and the Eight Great Bodhisattvas,
c. 1300–1400

Goryeo dynasty (918–1392). Hanging scroll, ink, colors, and gold on silk. $59\frac{1}{2} \times 34\frac{15}{16}$ in. The Avery Brundage Collection, B72D38

BOX 6099   ROHNERT PARK   CA 94927

Pomegranate